Meiji Japan

Harold Bolitho

Published in cooperation with Cambridge University Press
Lerner Publications Company, Minneapolis

Editors' Note: In preparing this edition of *The Cambridge Topic Books* for publication, the editors have made only a few minor changes in the original material. In some isolated cases, British spelling and usage were altered in order to avoid possible confusion for our readers. Whenever necessary, information was added to clarify references to people, places, and events in British history. An index was also provided in each volume.

In this book all Japanese names appear according to customary Japanese usage, with the family name first and the personal name last.

LIBRARY OF CONGRESS CATALOGING IN PUBLICATION DATA

Bolitho, Harold.
  Meiji Japan.

  (A Cambridge Topic Book)
  Includes index.
  SUMMARY: Examines the dramatic changes that occurred in Japan after diplomatic and economic relations were established with the West in 1853.

  1. Japan—History—Restoration, 1853-1870—Juvenile literature.
  2. Japan—History—Meiji period, 1868-1912—Juvenile literature.
  [1. Japan—History—Restoration, 1853-1870. 2. Japan—History—Meiji period, 1868-1912] I. Title.

DS881.3B64 1980   952'.025   80-7448
ISBN 0-8225-1219-X

This edition first published 1980 by Lerner Publications Company by permission of Cambridge University Press.

Original edition copyright © 1977 by Cambridge University Press as part of *The Cambridge Introduction to the History of Mankind: Topic Book*.

International Standard Book Number: 0-8225-1219-X
Library of Congress Catalog Card Number: 80-7448

Manufactured in the United States of America.

This edition is available exclusively from:
Lerner Publications Company, 241 First Avenue North, Minneapolis, Minnesota 55401

1 2 3 4 5 6 7 8 9 10 85 84 83 82 81 80

Contents

Japan in the mid-nineteenth century

Land over 500m (1640ft)
The Japanese Islands

0   km   1000
0   miles   500

RUSSIA

MONGOLIA

MANCHURIA

HOKKAIDO

KOREA

JAPAN

HONSHU

Kyoto   Edo

Osaka

SHIKOKU

CHINA

Nagasaki   KYUSHU

MACAO

BURMA   HONG KONG

PACIFIC

OCEAN

THAILAND

PHILIPPINE
ISLANDS

MALAY
STATES

EAST INDIES

front cover: *Exotic British goods on display at the British trading post in Yokohama. The print was designed in the 1860s by the artist Yoshiiku*

back cover: *There was much violence when the government changed in 1868. Here followers of the old regime are engaged in setting fire to the property of some supporters of the new. You can read about this on page 22.*

1 The coming of the West

Most countries of the world went through some sort of upheaval between the years 1600 and 1850. Britain and France each had revolutions, accompanied by bloodshed and disorder; colonies in both North and South America fought for, and won, their independence; a series of wars kept Europe in turmoil; in Africa and India great empires were built by men as ruthless as they were dedicated; the Manchus in China fought and overcame the Ming rulers. But the islands of Japan, in their remote corner of the Pacific, saw no such turbulence. For them, instead, the two and a half centuries after 1600 brought peace after many hundreds of years of civil war.

Ironically, that peace had been granted at last by the most pugnacious group in Japan. Ever since the twelfth century, groups of warriors – the *samurai* – had scrambled for power among themselves, each unwilling to give in to the other. Japan was split into warring states, constantly expanding and contracting according to the fortunes of war, until the year 1600, when a great battle gave victory to the Tokugawa family. Then, under the government of the Tokugawa ruler – invested by the emperor of Japan with the ancient title of *shogun*, or commander-in-chief – the samurai finally co-operated in establishing a new system of government, one which offered them security and privilege, and which gave to their fellow-countrymen – farmers, fishermen, traders, shopkeepers and priests – stability and fresh opportunities. All around the islands, Japanese merchants could begin to trade with each other on a scale never seen before, and on the land the farmers could settle down peacefully to the task of keeping themselves alive, and paying their taxes. Both could profit from the growth of cities: Edo (now Tokyo), which within a century came to have a million inhabitants; Osaka, a commercial centre where half a million people made their living; and Kyoto, the solid, prosperous capital, where the emperor lived within his palace.

There were, naturally, some stresses and strains, as there must be in any community of human beings. But, on the whole, people obeyed the laws, paid their taxes, and settled their disputes amicably. To the sailor from Gillingham, Will Adams, shipwrecked on the Japanese coast in 1600, Japan seemed a very pleasant place indeed. 'The People are good of nature', he wrote, 'courteous out of measure, and valiant in War . . . There is not in the World a land better governed by Civil Policy.'

Yet, as the Japanese knew, good government and peace were only possible so long as other countries left them alone. Any pressure from abroad would be followed inevitably by discontent at home. It was here that the Japanese were particularly fortunate. Elsewhere, throughout these years, the sea-borne empires of Spain, Portugal, the Netherlands and Britain arose and flourished. They might have taken in Japan, too, had it not been for three considerations. Japan was a very long way from Europe, and could be reached only after a sea journey covering half the world – the longest journey a European could imagine. Secondly, Japan had very little to tempt the Europeans, who were quite busy enough with the riches of the Americas, the Indies and Africa. Centuries before, Marco Polo had written of a land called Cipangu, where gold was found in quantities so vast that whole palaces were roofed with it, and where pearls were so abundant that they were crammed into the mouths of corpses. He was misinformed, as the first traders to reach Japan in the late sixteenth century were to discover. There was some gold and silver, but little else that could not be found much more readily closer to home.

For these two reasons, Europeans were largely indifferent to Japan. English merchants carried on some desultory trading, but finally closed their Japanese office in 1623. The Spanish and the Portuguese were formally expelled, but there was not enough business to interest them anyway. Only the Dutch stayed to carry on a trickle of trade with the Japanese, and they were penned up on a small spit of land at Nagasaki, itself the most distant of Japanese cities from the centre of Japan. If they ever set foot outside, it was only under armed escort.

Two contrasting views of Nagasaki, with the Dutch trading post on the crescent-shaped island in the foreground. At the top is a picture scroll painted in 1792 by the Japanese artist Maruyama Okyo. The picture below is from Nippon by von Siebold (1796–1866), a German physician and biologist. The European version makes the Dutch settlement seem much more important than the Japanese panorama does. Guards posted on the causeway prevented informal meetings between Dutch and Japanese.

The third reason was that the Japanese, no less than the Europeans, could not see very much profit in trade. There was little the Europeans produced that the Japanese needed—trinkets like clocks and clockwork toys were interesting, but no more; firearms they could make for themselves, after having learned the principle. Cloth from the Coromandel Coast in India and pepper from the East Indies were in some demand, but really the only foreign goods of any concern to the Japanese were the products of her closest neighbours, China and Korea—silks, brocades and medicinal herbs. Japan was also aware of the dangers of too close a contact with the empires of the West, where merchants, soldiers and missionaries all worked hand in hand for expansion. It was fear of just such foreign interference

which prompted the Tokugawa government, in the 1630s, to seal Japan off from foreign contact. The Spanish and Portuguese were ordered away, no Japanese was allowed travel abroad, and Christianity was forbidden.

By cutting off almost all contact with the Western world, the Japanese probably did secure over 200 years of peace for themselves. They paid a very great price, however. It was during Japan's isolation that Galileo, Kepler, Harvey, Newton, Lavoisier and Watt lived and worked; the world was in the middle of a scientific and technological revolution, and Japan remained – for the most part – ignorant of it. In the 1630s, the technology of Japan had not been so different from that of Europe, but by the mid-nineteenth century the Japanese had

These three men are dressed as samurai of the late Tokugawa period, with their traditional weapons of war.

been left far behind. A trickle of Dutch technical books had been imported since the early eighteenth century, but there was little chance for any practical demonstration of the wonders they described. Early Japanese botanists carried Dutch texts with them out into the forests; even a human dissection was performed, in 1771, by Japanese surgeons with Dutch books of anatomy in their hands. But how could a man who had never seen a blast furnace or a steam engine understand them from books alone? Japan's isolation put her at a disadvantage, and it was dangerous as well as inconvenient – dangerous simply because of advances in military technology. All Japan could muster in her own defence, against the newly developed rifle and the ironclad steamship, were small wooden junks, archaic cannon, and smooth-bore matchlock muskets.

Obviously, by 1850, the Japanese were not equipped to reopen relations with the West on equal terms. But from the beginning of the nineteenth century it became clear that, sooner or later, reopen they must. The Russians, who had gradually spread across Siberia, were naturally interested in exploring the seas and islands off their east coast. The Americans were active, too. Ever since the beginning of the century the United States had been vigorously involved in the China trade, and many of her 700 whaling vessels, sailing out of ports like Nantucket, eventually found their way to Japanese waters. The opening of California, and the growing use of the Sandwich (Hawaiian) Islands, together with the introduction of steamships to the Pacific, all served to bring Japan and the United States much closer. British merchants, too, trading in every commodity from opium to tea at the Chinese ports open to them by treaty, were drawn to the prospects of new markets just a few days' sail from Tientsin.

With all this increased traffic around their coast-line, it was simply a matter of time before the Japanese came to reconsider their policy of exclusion. At first, contact was informal, as some vessels were shipwrecked and others sent boats ashore for fresh

food and water. Then came formal attempts to establish diplomatic and trade relations with Japan. In 1793, and again in 1804, the Russians sent missions to their Japanese neighbours, but each was rebuffed. Some Americans made a private attempt in 1837, only to have their unarmed ship fired upon by Japanese coastal batteries; an official mission, led by Commodore James Biddle, was bluntly turned away (and Biddle himself jostled by a Japanese guard) in 1846.

In 1853 the Americans tried again, this time determined to succeed, with an expedition on which every care was lavished. On the evening of 8 July, four ships of the United States Navy dropped anchor at Uraga, just 40 miles (64 km) south of Edo,

Commodore Matthew Perry through Japanese and Western eyes. The Japanese artist was apparently not used to depicting either curly hair or epaulettes.

A Japanese impression of the steamship Powhatan. This was Perry's flagship during his second visit to Japan in 1854. It had a crew of 350, 21 medium guns and 8 large cannon.

the seat of Tokugawa government. Two of the vessels – the *Susquehanna* and the *Mississippi* – were steamships, at the sight of which Japanese fishermen stood up in awe in their boats, for they were the first ever seen in Japan. The two war sloops – *Saratoga* and *Plymouth* – which accompanied them were smaller, but just as overwhelming to the Japanese. To observers on shore, the four ships seemed as huge and threatening as 'floating castles'.

The expedition, which aimed at 'friendship, commerce, a supply of coal and provisions for our shipwrecked people', was in the care of Commodore Matthew Calbraith Perry, one of the most senior officers in the United States Navy. Then nearly sixty years old, Perry had had a long and fine naval career. So too had his father, his brother, his brothers-in-law, and a large number of cousins. He was, furthermore, no stranger to gunboat diplomacy, looking back with pride on 'former commands upon the coast of Africa, and in the Gulf of Mexico, where it fell to my lot to subjugate many towns and communities'.

He planned his Japanese mission with typical naval thoroughness and precision, first reading everything on Japan

he could find, and then questioning everybody with any information on the subject; from this he decided on a strategy. First of all, he foresaw that the Japanese would probably want to negotiate at Nagasaki, 800 miles (1,300 km) away from the major political centre at Edo. Instead, Perry insisted on conducting his business as close to Edo as possible, keeping the Japanese under pressure.

Then, too, the commodore refused to deal with any but officials of the highest rank, remaining concealed in his cabin for days on end while his subordinates acted as go-betweens. Japanese were allowed only on the flagship (and even then no more than three at any one time), and any other attempts to board were refused. Wisely, in anticipation of long delays, Perry had made certain of plentiful stores of food and water to enable him to wait it out.

Members of Perry's crew, as seen by a Japanese artist. On the left, a rifleman, one of the Marines whose military drill dazzled the Japanese. The other man is amusing himself with a Japanese banjo.

Japanese sumo wrestlers astonishing Perry with their feats of strength. Arauma ('Wild Horse'), in the centre of the picture, is carrying four bales of rice – a total weight of 500 pounds (227 kg). Commodore Perry, suitably astonished, is shown in the centre background.

Behind all the polite discussions, as both Perry and the Japanese were aware, was the threat of force. If no appropriate person was prepared to receive the documents he carried, then Perry made clear his intention to 'go onshore with sufficient force and deliver them in person, be the consequences what they might'. Local officials, who had noted the grim determination on the foreigners' faces, believed him, and in the end Perry had his way.

The Japanese, for their part, had been astounded to find the foreign ships at anchor – far more so than they had any right to be. For years there had been regular sightings of foreign ships, and the story of Britain's victory against China in the Opium War of 1840-2 had caused great concern in nearby Japan. The Dutch had warned them repeatedly of American action, and many coastal areas had been fortified with gun emplacements

as a result. Yet it was as if the appearance of Perry's 'black ships' (as the Japanese – impressed by the fact that they were painted black – called them) had come as a total surprise. No coherent policy had been developed, no troops appeared until the next day, and the Japanese seemed at a loss to know what to do. They were intensely curious, yes – boatloads of Japanese, maintaining a healthy distance, scouted around the ships, observing and sketching – and intensely afraid, for when it grew dark, bonfires lined the coast and the hilltops and a great bell tolled through the night. But their first official overture was to display a notice – in French – asking the ships to go away; when this did not work, the Japanese requested – this time in Dutch – that the Americans proceed to Nagasaki. Neither these, nor subsequent approaches, had any effect.

On 14 July the Japanese gave in, in a dignified ceremony –

In an exchange of gifts to commemorate the Treaty of Kanagawa (see page 11), the United States gave Japan samples of agricultural implements (like the scythe at the right) and a miniature railway engine.

or as dignified as any surrender can be, especially when held on a sandy beach on a fine summer's day. Perry handed over to Toda Ujihide, the local governor, a small wooden box containing a letter, on parchment, signed by President Millard Fillmore, thirteenth president of the United States. The letter was brief and to the point. After introducing the bearer (Perry) to the emperor of Japan (and informing the emperor just where and what the United States of America were), the president suggested that 'if your imperial majesty were so far to change the ancient laws as to allow a free trade between the two countries it would be extremely beneficial to both'. Perry added that he would return for an answer the following year – with an even larger fleet. Once again, the Japanese knew what he meant.

On 17 July 1853, Commodore Perry sailed to spend the rest of the summer and the autumn quietly in Macao; he left behind him a country in turmoil. The government was torn between its weakness and its pride, while the people alternated between friendly curiosity, and fear, hatred and mistrust. It was from such turmoil and confusion that a new Japan, led by a new government, was to emerge.

2 The end of Tokugawa Japan

Perry had left the Japanese with a problem. Would they say yes or no to the American demand? The choice that faced them was straightforward enough, but each alternative carried its own risks.

It was dangerous to do as the Americans wanted. Once Japan had opened to the United States, then Great Britain, France, Russia and the Netherlands would certainly want similar treatment, and so she would be pushed immediately into the turmoil of international diplomacy. Also, if Japan once gave in to a threat of force she might then become the target for more – and less reasonable – demands.

How, too, would she be able to cope with foreign trade? This was a big worry, since most people thought that the foreigners were interested only in robbing Japan of her treasures, forcing her to take worthless trade goods in return. Were foreigners to trade in Japan, one man wrote, 'It will be hard to maintain the laws of the Imperial Land, and our people will suffer; trade may benefit the foreigners, but can do us nothing but harm.'

Just as important, the ruler of Japan was the shogun, whose full title, bestowed on his ancestor by the Emperor Goyozei in 1603, meant Commander-in-Chief of the Pacification of Barbarians. It had been the duty of the shogun ever since to protect the emperor and his kingdom from precisely the kind of danger which now faced them. Giving in to foreign threats would be to admit that the Tokugawa shogun could no longer do the job. If he could not, then who could?

There was another problem, too. Japanese mythology, still widely accepted, held that the land and people of the Japanese islands were specially created by the gods, and were therefore more important than any others. The past 200 years of isolation had not shown them anything to make them change their minds. To bow down to inferior people from uncivilized countries like America and Britain – people who, it was rumoured, were so deformed that they could not bend the legs which they kept hidden by trousers – would be seen by many Japanese as unnatural. Possibly the Japanese people themselves might not stand for such a shameful betrayal of their divine heritage.

But what alternative was there? If the Tokugawa government said no, then quite clearly they would have to fight, and they were in no position to do that. The United States, with its enormous warships and its formidable firepower, would have no trouble with opponents whose weapons – swords, pikes, primitive muskets – were those of the seventeenth century, and who had not really used them since then.

The Japanese had no hope of defeating the barbarians under these circumstances. To try would be to invite a thrashing from which they would never recover, and give the foreign conquerors a free hand.

Neither course of action was very appetizing. But the choice had to be made, and made quickly, for Commodore Perry had promised to return for his answer the following year, 1854. The Tokugawa government, after asking the advice of local leaders throughout the country, made the only possible decision. Despite the urging of firebrands who believed that the gods would protect Japan in any war, or who thought that even certain defeat was better than cowardly submission, the Japanese government greeted Perry on his return with the Treaty of Kanagawa, which gave him nearly everything he wanted. Two new ports were to be opened to United States vessels, and the Japanese would now sell them fuel and provisions. At some future date each country would send the other a consul to help smooth relations between them.

The Japanese rather hoped that the matter would rest there. Certainly they would never have bothered sending a consul to New York, where they had no interests, and where they did not want any, either. The Americans, however, meant business, and in 1856 a man called Townsend Harris arrived at Shimoda to begin his duties as United States consul. Politely refusing the suggestion of the local Japanese governor that he might like to

go back home again, Harris set up house in a hillside temple and prepared for a long stay.

He needed every minute of it. His task was to get Japan and the United States trading with each other, and this took all his patience and cunning as he coaxed and threatened the Japanese into agreement. By 1858 he had won the Treaty of Shimoda from them, and Japan was now open for business.

The Treaty of Shimoda, and similar arrangements with the Netherlands, Britain, France and Russia which followed a few months later, were not at all favourable to the Japanese. They had never wanted to trade. Now they were forced to, and foreign businessmen were to be allowed to come and go freely in six Japanese ports, living there under their own laws, with their

left: *Townsend Harris, first United States consul to Japan.*

below: *Harris and Heusken (his interpreter, who was later murdered), escorted by a censor and the Shimoda magistrate, go to visit the shogun in 1858.*

An English artist's impression of the customs house at Yokohama in 1861. You can see Japanese officials and porters, a European businessman, and a Chinese servant.

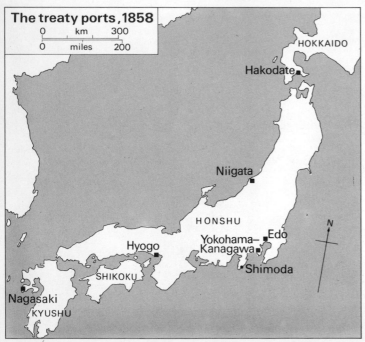

The treaty ports, 1858

km 0 — 300
miles 0 — 200

HOKKAIDO

Hakodate

Niigata

HONSHU

Hyogo

Yokohama—
Kanagawa

Edo

Shimoda

SHIKOKU

Nagasaki

KYUSHU

N

own police and their own military protection. Japanese who went abroad to trade, however, were not given the same privileges. The Tokugawa government was also forced to accept foreign goods almost duty-free.

The treaties were tremendously unpopular. This was not because they were unfair. In fact they were, but the Japanese did not realize it for some time. They were unpopular because they had been forced on the Japanese against their will, and by alien people. Many would have shared the feelings of the samurai who criticized his country's capitulation in a bitter couplet:

Now the Japanese sword is tarnished,
And the warrior's spirit broken.

To some samurai the only way to avenge the insult was by violence to individual foreigners – 'to chop them up like radishes', as one hothead said – when they began to arrive from 1860 onwards. The next few years saw attacks – some fatal – on officials and businessmen from abroad. Henry Heusken, a young Dutch interpreter who had come to Japan with Townsend Harris, was hacked to death by a swordsman in 1861. The following year, C. L. Richardson, an English

below: *The foreign settlement at Yokohama, with its strange vehicles, stranger buildings and (if one can believe this wood-block print) even stranger flags, was an object of considerable curiosity to the Japanese.*

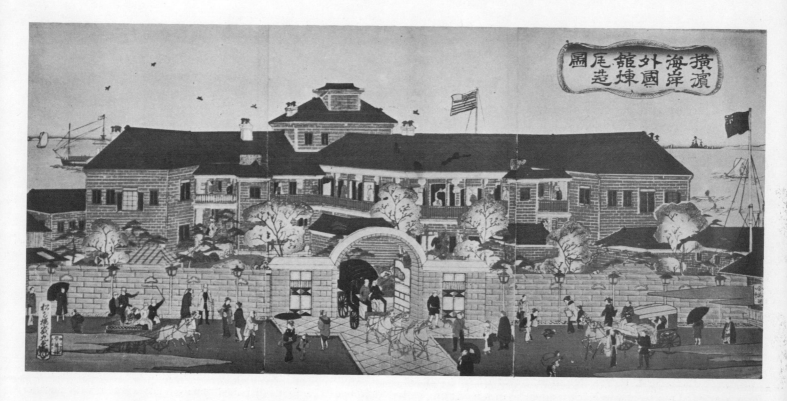

businessman, out riding with some companions near the little village of Namamugi near Yokohama, encountered the escort of a prominent political figure and was cut down on the spot.

If the foreigners and their treaties were unpopular, then the government which had capitulated to them was even more so. Tokugawa Japan had its tensions, and the natural human reflex was to blame the government. The samurai class, in particular, had complaints, for the peace, prosperity and commercial opportunities of the Tokugawa period seemed to them not really suited to their traditions. Jealous of their family heritage,

proud of their skills with sword and brush, and disdainful alike of 'stupid' peasants and 'greedy' businessmen, the samurai really lived in another world. They had failed to keep pace with the rest of society.

So, too, had the governments, central and provincial, in which the samurai served. The result was friction, between one class and another, and one government and another, and this was increasingly expressed in criticism of the central government, the Tokugawa *bakufu*. As the nineteenth century wore on there were complaints that the Tokugawa house ruled Japan for its own benefit, and did not care about the general welfare.

There were other complaints that the government was too repressive, too demanding, too high-handed, and run by people who were simply not clever enough. Perry's arrival, and the government's obvious confusion, sharpened and increased that criticism. The shogun had failed, it was said. He could not resist the foreigners, he could not protect the people, and he could not protect the emperor.

It was, of course, true. Worried by the criticism and needing support, the Tokugawa bakufu invited some of its major critics, like one kinsman Tokugawa Nariaki, the peppery baron of Mito, into its ranks as special advisers, but this failed to do any good. The result was not so much to appease the critics, who began to sense that they were winning, as to confuse and paralyse a government already indecisive and frightened. A sign of its perplexity was the rapid turnover of government officials, who, as one contemporary said, 'are appointed in the morning and resign the same night'.

The Tokugawa government was open to attack on another side as well. People unhappy with the shogun could always turn to the emperor, for the shogun was, in theory at least, the emperor's servant. Japanese mythology gave a particular divinity to the emperor, held to be a direct descendant of the Sun Goddess herself. It was this man, never stirring outside the grounds of his palace in Kyoto, never so much as glimpsed by his subjects, normally never consulted on the running of the country, who alone could protect those who openly criticised the government. If he wanted to, the emperor could help to change the direction of national policy.

Fortunately for the critics, and unfortunately for the Tokugawa house, the Emperor Komei (1831-66) did want to. Having never once set eyes on a foreigner (for that matter he had seen very few Japanese), he had no wish to do so. He had been reliably informed that these barbarians from across the seas looked like animals, and he wanted nothing to do with them. So he had broken a 200-year tradition of imperial silence, and announced his contempt for foreigners 'who resemble birds and beasts', and his displeasure with a government which could meekly obey such savages.

He did not leave matters there. In fact, he went on to refuse his consent to the treaties, and to call openly on his subjects to drive the barbarians away. The bakufu, with its back to the wall, had to override him on the first issue, and ignore him on the second, but it paid a heavy price. Those who opposed the Tokugawa house could now claim, with some accuracy, that they represented the emperor's wishes – no matter how unrealistic those wishes were – more than did the government. In the fighting which was soon to break out they could label themselves 'loyalists'.

below: *In 1867 the country was amazed by rumours of coins and amulets falling from the sky. As a result, many thousands of people decided to set off on pilgrimages. The print is by the artist Yoshiiku who also designed the picture on the front cover.*

All of this took place in an atmosphere of general anxiety and unease. The emperor was being insulted, foreigners were defiling the imperial land, prices were rising, and there was a typhoid epidemic. Large numbers of farmers in western Japan were leaving their fields and setting off on a spontaneous pilgrimage to the sacred shrine at Ise, leaving turmoil behind them. In the cities there were riots (over forty separate incidents during the summer of 1866) as the poor plundered the storehouses of the rich. All over Japan young samurai were quitting their homes to gather in Edo and Kyoto and plot violence against the foreigners and those Japanese leaders who seemed sympathetic to them. Kyoto, the placid old imperial city, was in an uproar, with fighting in the streets, and pitched battles at the very gates of the emperor's palace. 'At night there are robbers in the streets', wrote a samurai visiting the city in 1866, 'there are murders, there are burglary, arson, suicide, infanticide and beheadings, every night.'

The combination of unrest and opposition made the Tokugawa government very much weaker. But in fact it had never been particularly strong. It had endured for 250 years, and had given Japan peace, but to do so it had always relied on a precarious balance of power. Only 20% of the country paid taxes to the Tokugawa shogun; the remainder was ruled by some 260 barons, who paid no taxes to the government, and obeyed its instructions only when it suited them. The larger barons (or *daimyo*) had armies of their own, and, inside their domains, were largely independent of the government far away in Edo.

Under normal circumstances, the balance of power between the government and the barons was secure enough. The arrangement suited both sides, and each knew that to upset it would only start a new round of dangerous (and expensive) civil wars. But this was only in normal circumstances.

After 1853 and Perry nothing was normal, for Japan's leaders had discovered that their habitual relations with each other,

In 1860 a party of Japanese officials was taken across the Pacific in a Japanese vessel, the Kanrin-maru, under Japanese command. It was an ambitious voyage, but a successful one, even though the captain was too seasick to take much part in it. The journey took 37 days and met with rough weather.

below: Members of the party turned their sketching abilities to good use, as in this shipboard view of a remarkably oriental San Francisco.

below: *A picture, from the same voyage, of a San Francisco street scene, showing high-stepping horses and a high-stepping gentleman.*

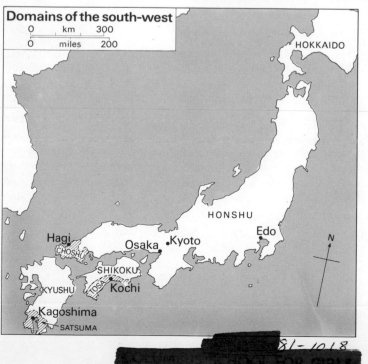

Domains of the south-west

0   km   300
0   miles   200

HOKKAIDO

HONSHU

Hagi
CHOSHU
Osaka • Kyoto
Edo

N

SHIKOKU
KYUSHU   TOSA   Kochi

Kagoshima
SATSUMA

their traditional way of life, their customary military strength, and their usual finances, were no longer enough. The barons needed to pay more attention to their own defence, and they needed more money to buy weapons. The Tokugawa government, on the other hand, with its national responsibilities, wanted more help from the barons than they would give. These incompatible demands shattered the old stability.

There were unmistakable signs that the old order had broken down. One by one the barons went their own way, and the central government, humiliated by Perry and criticized on all sides, could no longer stop them. In south-western Japan in particular, the barons – and their samurai advisers – were reaching out for greater independence, in a movement which was finally to pull the Tokugawa bakufu down. The south-west had always been rather more independent than the rest of Japan. It was, after all, a long way from Edo, Osaka and Kyoto, the main centres of Tokugawa power. Also, since it was closer than any other part of Japan to international shipping routes, and used to the sight of foreign ships, it was considerably more nervous about its own safety, and more concerned to buy weapons to defend itself. So, although private diplomacy and trade (especially the purchase of weapons) with the foreigners were illegal, the domains of the south-west were deeply involved in both after the trade treaty of 1858. There was no other way for them to obtain modern weapons, nor was there any other way for them to earn the money such weapons cost.

Three of the south-western domains stood out in this movement. Satsuma, the powerful domain in southern Kyushu, led by barons of the Shimazu family since the end of the twelfth century, was one. It had its difficulties with the foreigners, notably in mid-1863, when it was bombarded by six British warships in retaliation for the murder of Richardson (see page 14). Basically, however, its baron and his advisers welcomed the prospect of trade, building a sugar refinery, a paper factory, a tannery, a glue factory, as well as blast furnaces, in an effort to

19

produce something the West might buy. It was successful. An observer in 1866 noted that 'Satsuma is steadily growing into a strong province, with a powerful army; it has imported Western weapons, and four or five foreign instructors, and drills its troops incessantly.'

Choshu, a domain which sprawled over two provinces at the western end of Honshu, was another. The baron, Mori Takachika, while not outstanding himself, was served—some said led—by some of the most forceful and determined samurai in Japan. They were also anti-foreign. When the emperor ordered that foreigners were to be expelled after 24 June 1863, Choshu was the only domain to obey, firing at foreign shipping in the straits of Shimonoseki. In retaliation a combined fleet of British, American, French and Dutch vessels launched an attack on Choshu which destroyed its coastal batteries, and converted its leaders promptly to a more moderate policy. From 1865 onwards they busily bought up as many Western ships and guns as they could afford, and tried to earn money through candle-making, paper-making, weaving and dyeing.

The third of these domains was Tosa, on the Pacific coast of Shikoku, an area renowned for its good fish and its bad-tempered people. At this time it was also well known for the personality and talents of its baron, Yamauchi Yodo. Despite his fondness for the bottle – he boasted that he was drunk 360 days a year – it was his energy which brought Tosa to the political forefront. His domain, like Satsuma and Choshu, was set on developing its local industries – whaling, and the making of paper and camphor-oil – and buying up as many armaments as it could afford.

In combination, these three domains presented a formidable spearhead. All close to each other, all with similar problems, together they held a substantial amount of land, and acquired nearly as many modern warships as the bakufu itself. Their difficulty lay in agreeing to combine, for while they distrusted the Tokugawa bakufu, they mistrusted each other rather more. All three domains were extremely active in internal Japanese politics, where they were already jockeying for influence early in the 1850s. Beginning with secret (and illegal) attempts to win the emperor's approval, by messages of support and gifts of money, all three finally moved into the central arena. Both Satsuma and Tosa tried, successfully, to force the central government to moderate its demands, give the barons more freedom, and so weaken itself still further.

By the 1860s it had become clear that the old form of government could not survive; it had failed to cope with the outside world, and it could no longer control the barons. People were accordingly obliged to consider new forms of government. When they did, three possibilities emerged. One was that the Tokugawa shogun could make himself stronger, and the country more united, by getting rid of the troublesome barons, and claiming control not of 20% of the country, but of 100%. If necessary he could call on a foreign nation – perhaps the French – for help. Another possibility – favoured by both Satsuma and Tosa – was that the government could surrender some of its power to the barons, and co-operate with them in running Japan, rather as King John of England had promised to do at Runnymede, long ago. The third option, supported vociferously and violently by Choshu, was that the Tokugawa government could be replaced by something more or less the same, only stronger, and run by different people. Whatever happened, Japan needed a stronger government to hold the country together as it confronted the outside world.

What finally brought the domains together was the threat of the first of these possibilities, when the bakufu in 1865 suddenly announced a reform programme, began negotiations for French aid, and ordered the destruction of Choshu, where its most dangerous critics were. Few barons could approve of such brutal treatment for one of their number. Both Satsuma and Tosa opposed it openly, Satsuma to the extent of allying with Choshu in its resistance. When the government's reform plans failed, and the campaign against Choshu ground humiliatingly

Tokugawa Yoshinobu.

to a halt, Tokugawa Yoshinobu, who was then the shogun, took the only possible way out. Late in 1867 he accepted a Tosa proposal that he resign.

By resigning, Yoshinobu thought to take his place at the head of a council of nobles. Had he done so, he would have been by far its most influential member, simply because no other baron held nearly as much land. He was due for a shock. Satsuma and Choshu, now in combination, saw their chance to topple the government and take power for themselves. This they did, helped by sympathetic courtiers, in a *coup d'état*.

On the morning of 3 January 1868, in the emperor's palace in

Satsuma's part in the coup d'état of January 1868 was resented in Edo, where bakufu troops responded by burning down Satsuma offices.

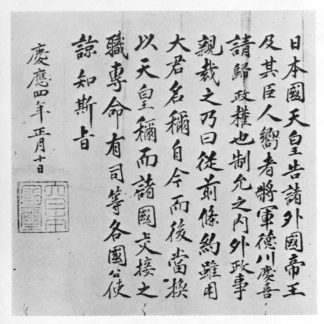

This notice informed foreign diplomats of the change in government.

Kyoto, surrounded by armed guards from Satsuma and elsewhere, a spokesman for the emperor announced the outlines of a new form of government. The office of shogun was to be abolished, and the Tokugawa house punished for its misrule by having its lands – and its income – confiscated. Government was to return to the pattern set down at the very birth of the Japanese state: the emperor himself, assisted by advisers, was to rule. The Tokugawa bakufu was at an end.

Within a few days the emperor's new troops – most of them from Satsuma and Choshu – had driven pro-Tokugawa forces out of the Kyoto–Osaka area, and set off eastwards towards Edo, to take control of the city built by the Tokugawa house nearly 300 years before. As they marched they sang a new song:

My prince, my prince,
What flutters by your steed?
Toko ton yare
It is a brocade banner,
With which to end all treason.
Toko ton yare.

3 The new government

Ten months after the troops marched off singing, their emperor followed them, escorted by 3,000 men. On the ornate carriage in which he rode was perched a gilt phoenix, the mythical bird whose appearance was said to foretell a reign of outstanding brilliance. The symbol was aptly chosen, for the next forty years were to be just that.

Yet it was questionable how much the emperor himself contributed. The year 1868 marked a Restoration in his name, by people claiming to wish nothing more than to serve him, but he was to remain as much a symbol as the mythical phoenix. The Emperor Komei had died in 1866, and the throne had passed to his young son, the fifteen-year-old Mutsuhito. Born and raised in isolation, he was totally inexperienced, and so hardly likely to take charge of the complex business of government himself. Nor were the tough-minded men around him likely to allow any such thing. As they reminded each other cynically, by controlling the emperor they had 'stolen the jewel', the magic talisman by which miracles could be worked, and they intended to use it.

The emperor was to be their symbol of national unification. This, in fact, was why he was leaving Kyoto, where his ancestors had lived for a thousand years, to take up residence in the busy seaport of Edo (by now renamed Tokyo, or Eastern Capital, in preparation for his arrival). The move was aimed at giving him a prominence and a public visibility undreamt of by any previous emperor. This was absolutely essential. If it was to

The emperor's carriage sets off, October 1868.

survive, let alone accomplish anything, the new government needed the goodwill which only the emperor could bring.

The Meiji government suffered from three severe handicaps. In the first place, only half a dozen of the 260 domains had joined in the *coup d'état*. The rest, while far from happy under the old government, were uneasy with the new. It was obvious that Satsuma and Choshu dominated the army and the imperial guard. It was also obvious that, despite the emperor's promise to establish a 'widely convoked' assembly which would decide policy by 'public discussion', the government was really run by some twenty men. Not unnaturally, most of these also came from Satsuma and Choshu, making the fiction of a 'national' government hard to sustain.

Secondly, there were the men themselves. They were politicians of a new sort. In the past, government had been the preserve of the elderly and the high-born. Now the nation's leaders were quite young. Saigo Takamori, at forty, was one of the oldest; Okubo Toshimichi was thirty-eight, Kido Takayoshi was thirty-five, and Ito Hirobumi only twenty-seven. They were also quite poor. The most any one of them could have hoped to become under the old government was a minor provincial official.

It was the crisis of the 1850s which had made their energy and ability valuable. Saigo, burly, hard-drinking and impatient, and the thin, puritanical and cool Okubo were both Satsuma men. Saigo the diplomat brought Satsuma and Choshu together in 1866; Okubo the strategist pulled off the *coup d'état* in 1868; Saigo the soldier controlled the army; Okubo the bureaucrat organized the new state; Saigo the bully threatened anybody who stood in the way. It was a remarkable com-

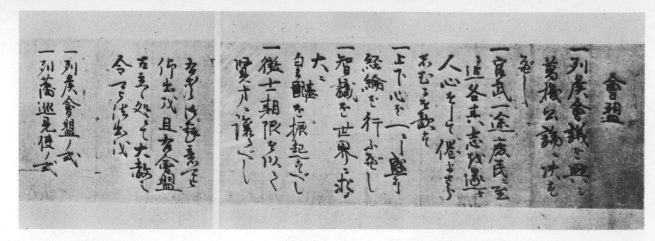

right: *A draft of the emperor's Charter Oath of 1868. The fourth clause promises to 'search the world for knowledge'.*

below: *Kido Takayoshi.*

bination. On the Choshu side, Kido Takayoshi was the compromiser and the peace-maker. Ito Hirobumi, also from Choshu, began his long political career by setting fire to the British Legation. He ended it fifty years later, after having served as Home Minister, Foreign Minister, four times as Prime Minister, and Governor-General of Korea.

These national leaders and their colleagues all had to give orders to men who were older, richer and more experienced —among them 260 barons. Had they not seemed to speak for the emperor, they would have been ignored.

The third handicap lay in the kind of orders these men gave. These were revolutionary, and in a few years had changed the whole shape and direction of Japanese society. There was resistance, but to oppose the reforms really seemed to mean opposing the emperor.

Change was associated, from the outset, with the new emperor's reign. In 1868, a year after his succession, the emperor's title or reign name was altered from the rather passive Keio, or Happiness Accomplished, to one much more assertive—Meiji, or Enlightened Government. Emperor Meiji had fixed his seal to a document promising to 'search the world for knowledge'. The seal was his, but the words were Kido's. Despite their own past prejudices, Kido and Okubo had decided on a wide variety of reforms. To cope successfully with the foreigners, protect their country from further demands, and win back the independence that had been given away with the treaties, the men from Satsuma and Choshu wanted to learn everything they could about the West. This was the only way to make their country stronger.

below: *Ito Hirobumi, towards the end of his life.*

Tophatted members of the Japanese government in San Francisco, 1872. Kido is seated on the left, Okubo Toshimichi on the right. The young man standing on the right is Ito Hirobumi. In the centre is Iwakura Tomomi, leader of the delegation.

So, in 1871, forty-eight members of the new government – Okubo, Kido and Ito among them – went overseas to see for themselves the countries which had bullied them out of isolation. Others followed, and in the next few years the cities of Europe and America were filled with parties of Japanese, notebooks in hand, observing, sketching and asking questions. Technology, economics, diplomacy, society, education – whatever the Western nations had, the visitors wanted to see it.

Within a few short years the new government developed an army and a police force modelled along Prussian lines, a British-style navy, and a French-style legal system. By 1871 the Japanese were employing almost 400 foreign advisers, brought over on generous salaries to show how to set about doing the thousand-and-one things the Japanese needed to know. Brewers from Bavaria, pastry-cooks from Paris, engineers from Edinburgh, teachers of everything from art to zoology, all came to Japan in the early years of the Meiji period to share their skills with eager young Japanese.

Kido and Okubo had seen that much in the West could be useful if copied at home. One example of this was government itself. As they looked at foreign countries they could see no system remotely like their own. Neither Britain nor the United States, for example, had independent barons collecting their own taxes, conducting their own foreign affairs and commanding their own armies. Japan had to be unified and centralized, no matter what the cost, and the Meiji government set out to do this.

Each of the major provincial cities had its impressive new school buildings, like this one at Matsumoto on the island of Honshu. It was built in the early 1870s.

By 1871 all the barons had been pensioned off (whether they liked it or not), and their armies and arsenals had been nationalized. Public servants, sent out by the government in Tokyo, took their place. Within a few years the map of Japan was completely transformed from a confused patchwork of domains into a regular arrangement of provinces and municipalities. The men from Satsuma and Choshu had ordered their own domains, as well as all the others, out of existence.

Japanese society also presented the new government with a serious problem. In the Tokugawa period everybody had believed that there were two kinds of men, the rulers and the ruled. The group you belonged to was that into which you happened to be born. If your father was a commoner, then you followed him in whatever his occupation was, whether farming (which accounted for 80% of the people), a skilled craft of some sort, or the business of buying, selling and money-lending. If you were lucky enough to be born into a warrior family, you would automatically become a samurai, responsible for ruling and protecting the common people, and, since this involved a

lot of training, you were paid a lifetime salary, whether or not you actually had a job. Simply being a samurai was a career in itself.

Okubo and Kido, as they looked around the world, soon saw the disadvantages of this sort of society. It was not a question of whether it was right or wrong: the point was that it was not very efficient. No modern state could afford to neglect bright young men simply because they had not been born into the samurai class. Talent was much more important than who your father was, and to make the best use of the talents of each Japanese the old class system had to be broken down. This was done in several ways.

First, the common people were allowed to use surnames, formerly a samurai privilege. Then they were allowed to choose for themselves what work they would do, so that a farmer's boy with a good business or administrative mind would not be forced to spend his life bent over his paddy fields, but could sell his land and go into commerce or government. To help him get the education he needed, the government built primary schools

: *Traditional Japanese barbers. The barber on the right is oiling his customer's hair before shaping it into a topknot like the ones in the pictures on pages 9 and 14. Such barbers were to be challenged by the new western hairstyles of the 1870s. They were finally put out of business by the prohibition of the topknot.*

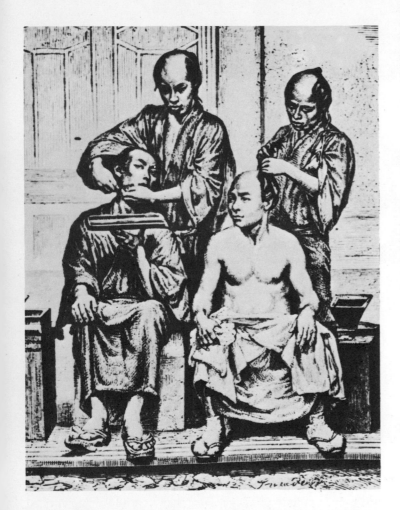

arrogant, touchy and quick to resort to violence. The new government had taken responsibility for them, only to discover that their salaries alone ate up more than half of the national revenue. It could not afford them.

So the government, themselves samurai, destroyed them – not as individuals, but as a class. The swaggering samurai, with his special dress, special hairstyle, and two swords at his belt, was swallowed up into a world where people dressed as they chose, where Tokyo could offer the services of 600 Western-style barbers' shops, and where only members of the police force and the new national army were allowed to go around armed. Samurai saw their salaries reduced, and in 1876 they were given lump-sum pensions, and turned out to fend for themselves.

The army was changed, too. As long as the samurai monopolized military skills, the new government could never be secure. It had become apparent in the 1860s that the samurai were too weak and inefficient to protect Japan from foreign enemies. But they were still strong enough to make things uncomfortable for any government they objected to. Therefore in 1872 Okubo and Kido, helped by Yamagata Aritomo, another Choshu man, started to develop a new army. It was to be made of conscripts, not samurai.

From all over the country, and from all walks of life, young men over the age of twenty-one were called up to spend three years in some distant barracks. They learned to fight with modern weapons, saw something of the rest of Japan, and finally went back to the shop or the farm having seen much more of the world than their fathers ever had. Instead of obeying an erratic baron, or an involved code of vendetta, these new Japanese soldiers – like their counterparts all over Europe – would be trained to serve their sovereign, the government and their nation.

The reforms, and the lightning speed with which they were carried out, were the real revolution of Meiji Japan. Ten years

throughout the country, and, in 1872, made education compulsory. Then there was the problem of the samurai. What was to be done with the two million of them, who made up nearly 7% of the total population? Many did no work at all, few had enough to keep them busy, and all were inclined to be

after the Tokugawa had been toppled, a new state had been built. Japan had become a country ruled by one central government, with a civil service and a national army. It was also about to begin Westernization in many other important fields.

Yet the reformers had themselves once been anti-foreign samurai, unable to see further than their own domains. Stranger still, they had made a modern nation in the name of the most ancient of Japanese symbols, the emperor.

4 The new life

For many Japanese, Meiji Japan was a brilliant and exciting place to live in. For the first time in their lives people were free of all the trivial restrictions of the Tokugawa period. They were free to do what they liked, go where they wished, and dress as they pleased. They could meet with people from all over the country – even with foreigners – and read books which previously would have been forbidden.

The result of this freedom was an amazing outpouring of creative energies as the Japanese took advantage of their new world. There were new life styles and a new culture to be enjoyed, and new ways of making the money needed to enjoy them. The Meiji period stands out as a golden age of Japanese history. Its catch-cry was *bunmei kaika*, civilization and enlightenment. Both seemed possible, and both were won.

Naturally, many of the older generation were offended by what seemed to them to be an aimless desire for change. One elderly general grumbled about his fellow-countrymen who, having 'made America their father and France their mother, are thoughtlessly changing old habits and customs'. But to the younger generation this was the best possible antidote to the dismay and confusion of the years which followed the Perry visit.

Certainly the new world offered enterprising young men a chance to get ahead. The government encouraged industrial development, for it had not escaped their notice that the strongest nations in the world were also the richest, and that they had grown rich through industry, not agriculture. So they gave tax concessions to industry, and also did their best to set an example.

To encourage production of silk for export, the government built a silk-spinning mill in the little country town of Tomioka. Instructors were recruited from France, and girls invited from all over Japan to learn the most efficient way of turning cocoons into silk thread. To cut down on imports, which was just as necessary as increasing exports, other factories were built near

An Englishman with his Chinese servant in Yokohama, portrayed in a popular print made by the Japanese artist Sadahide in 1866.

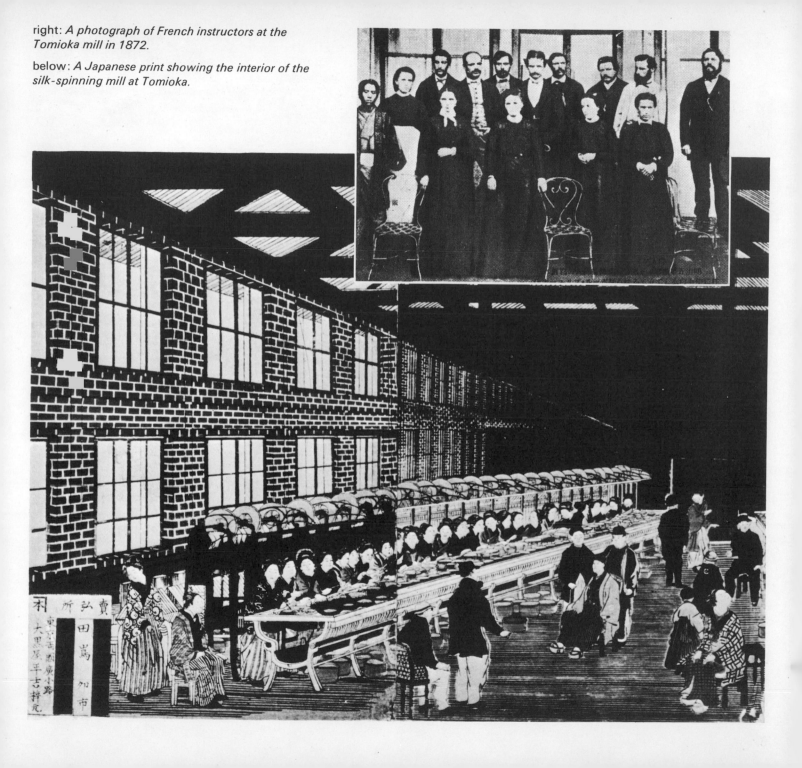

right: *A photograph of French instructors at the Tomioka mill in 1872.*

below: *A Japanese print showing the interior of the silk-spinning mill at Tomioka.*

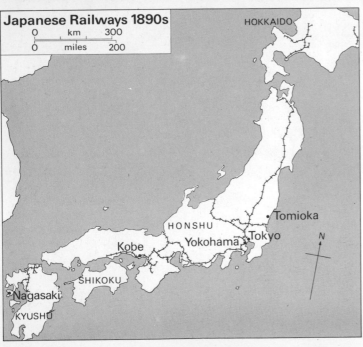

Japanese Railways 1890s

HOKKAIDO

HONSHU

Tomioka

Tokyo

Kobe

Yokohama

SHIKOKU

Nagasaki

KYUSHU

N

Japan's first railway, between Tokyo and Yokohama. In the picture on the left a steam engine at Yokohama is drawn with more imagination than observation. The first 18 miles of railway track were opened in 1872. The engines and the equipment came from England.

below: *The first Japanese-made steam locomotive, built in 1895.*

Tokyo to teach the Japanese how to meet their own needs. A glass-making factory at Shinagawa and a cement works at Fukagawa were just two examples of this.

Even more important to industrial development was the government's readiness to provide the public facilities that industry needed – railways, a postal system (started in 1871), a telegraph network (which by 1877 covered a distance upwards of 7,000 miles, or 11,000 kilometres) and even a telephone system, as well as good roads, bridges and port facilities. By 1882 Western industry had begun to catch on in Japan, where more than 2,000 factories were employing some 60,000 workers.

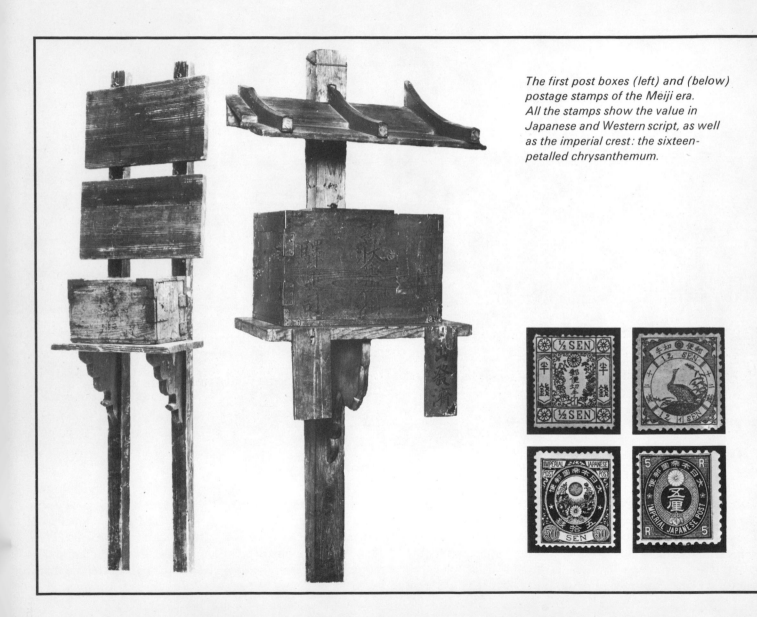

The first post boxes (left) and (below) postage stamps of the Meiji era. All the stamps show the value in Japanese and Western script, as well as the imperial crest: the sixteen-petalled chrysanthemum.

right: *The First National Bank, established 1872.*

below right: *A 10-yen banknote issued in 1881. The design was commissioned from an Italian, Edoardo Chiossone. It includes the imperial chrysanthemum and a portrait of the legendary Empress Jingu who was said to have conquered Korea.*

below left: *Iwasaki Yataro (1834-1885).*

Japanese businessmen were moving into all sorts of unfamiliar activities, from the dairy industry on the one hand to the production of safety matches on the other. The Meiji period had its share of rags-to-riches millionaires. Iwasaki Yataro, the shipping magnate and founder of the huge Mitsubishi organization, was one who, from modest origins as a country samurai, built up a fortune by using his wits. He also used government contacts, of which he had many, and once persuaded the government to buy thirteen steamships and lend them to him free of charge. Another from a small-town background was Shibusawa Eiichi, who used his financial skill first to become president of the First National Bank, and then to build up interests in some 500 companies, in fields as diverse as cotton-spinning and paper pulp.

below: *Japanese leaders and foreign diplomats mixing socially at the Rokumeikan official reception rooms. Ballroom dancing was unknown and unthinkable to Japanese society. One of the many sacrifices officials had to make for their country was learning how to do it. The picture is by a Western artist.*

below: *Fashionable young ladies. One is wearing European clothes, the other wears traditional Japanese dress, a contrast to be seen in many of the pictures in this book. A picture by a Japanese artist, 1890.*

By the 1880s Japan had grown accustomed to foreigners. She should have, since there were about 3,000 foreign residents, no longer huddled in foreign concessions (see page 13). There were large business communities in Yokohama, Kobe and Nagasaki, a very sprightly diplomatic set, devoted to dancing and parties, in Tokyo itself, and large numbers of missionaries and travellers in the interior. It was not unusual for Japanese schoolchildren to be taught by teachers from the United States and Great Britain – some missionaries, some not – while, if they went on to study at one of the many universities in Tokyo, it was even more likely that their instructors would come from the world outside. Lectures at the Tokyo Imperial University (founded by the government in 1877) were mainly in English, although the Faculty of Medicine, where German doctors held sway, preferred the German language, prompting British residents to snigger about the 'German measles' afflicting the Japanese medical profession.

Contact with foreign ideas, too, had become a commonplace,

left: *Kuroda Kiyoteru's* Lakeside, *painted in 1897. Artist and subject were Japanese, but the style was unmistakeably foreign.*

below: *By contrast with the picture above, this Japanese artist's view of an imaginary London was foreign in subject, but Japanese in style. The artist was Yoshitora, who was popular in the mid-nineteenth century.*

helped by the growth of the Japanese printing industry. Within twenty years of the first appearance of a Japanese newspaper in 1872, there were more than 600 different papers and magazines being published regularly. Here, and in translations of foreign works, the Japanese could meet with a wide range of new ideas. Samuel Smiles, whose *Self-Help* was translated into Japanese in 1871, taught them the virtues of self-reliance and initiative, while John Stuart Mill's *On Liberty*, translated the following year, informed them, to their amazement, that human beings had rights as well as obligations. Wordsworth showed them that Westerners also could love nature; Dickens, to their

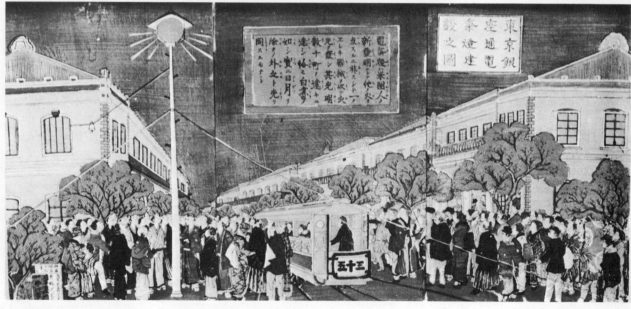

embarrassment, told them of romantic love between men and women.

Even Christianity, prohibited in Japan since the seventeenth century, became part of the Meiji intellectual world as missionaries were admitted once more. By 1885 there were 168 churches scattered about the Japanese islands, serving 11,000 converts whose influence in education and politics far outweighed their numbers.

right: *The Ginza, Tokyo's business district, in 1873. The artist has distorted the perspective so that a railway and ships seem to be hovering above the town. The original picture is in the Tokyo Metropolitan Central Library.*

below: *The Tokyo Central Tabernacle, a Christian church opened in 1891. Most denominations sent missionaries to Japan.*

In Japanese culture, too, the Western influence opened many avenues for writers and painters hungry for new sources of inspiration. The novelists of the Meiji period were all influenced by their readings of French, Russian and English novels, and many travelled abroad. For Japanese artists, just beginning to experiment with oils and with unfamiliar technical effects like perspective, light and shade, a trip to Paris, where they could wear their berets self-consciously and sit about the cafés, became an essential apprenticeship.

Few parts of Japanese life were unmarked by foreign contact. The little country towns were left largely unchanged, but in the streets of the larger cities old Japan had all but disappeared within twenty years of the Restoration. Imposing Western buildings, often designed by foreign architects, appeared. Horses and carriages could be seen, too, and later the horse-drawn tram; there were even gas lights in some streets by 1874.

The people, too, had changed. For one thing, their food was now far more varied than ever before. The rather monotonous diet of Tokugawa Japan – rice, pickled radish, soy bean products and green tea – was now enlivened by strange foods like apples, grapes, strawberries, cauliflowers and asparagus. Even meat slowly came to be accepted, despite its unfamiliar taste and its (for Buddhists) unpleasant origins. Networks of slaughter houses and butchers' shops sprang up to cater for those who would risk nausea rather than be unfashionable. Fortunately there was no such difficulty with the taste of beer

The Sapporo Brewery,
opened in 1876

right: *Japanese industry,*
trade and communication
developed rapidly throughout
the Meiji period.

Japanese steamships (merchant fleet)		Raw silk production		Coal production	
		(annual averages)		1875	600,000 metric tons
1873	26	1868–72	1,026 tons	1885	1,200,000
1894	169	1883	1,687	1895	5,000,000
1904	797	1889–93	4,098	1905	13,000,000
1913	1,514	1899–1903	7,103	1913	21,300,000
		1909–13	12,460		

Railway mileage		Raw silk export	
1872	18	(annual averages)	
1883	240	1868–72	646 tons
1887	640	1883	1,347
1894	2,100	1889–93	2,444
1904	4,700	1899–1903	4,098
1914	7,100	1909–13	9,462

(the first locally made bottle of which was opened in 1873) and whisky, both of which achieved instantaneous popularity.

The young emperor himself gave the lead in other changes. In 1873 he appeared dressed in trousers and jacket, instead of the clumsy pantaloons favoured by his ancestors for a thousand years, and with his hair cut and parted in the Western style, not arranged in a topknot. His army followed his example, finding the short haircut and tight-fitting tunic more suitable to military life than the elaborate coiffure and flowing robes of the samurai. Before long most Japanese were wearing at least some article of Western clothing – no matter how inappropriate it was to the rest of their costume, like a bowler hat or shoes worn with a kimono – to prove how enlightened they were. Certainly the situation had changed since 1863, when a Japanese returning from San Francisco with a neatly-furled umbrella as a memento of his visit was advised not to carry it in public unless he was prepared to risk assassination.

Japan had literally become a nation on the move. Freedom to go into the cities, the chance of finding work there, and conscription into the army, meant that people no longer were forced to live out their lives in their native village. Girls went off to work in factories until such time as their parents had found husbands for them, while farmers arrived during the slack season to earn extra money. Government railway construction, which had provided Japan with 5,000 miles (8,000 km) of track by the end of the century, placed long journeys within the reach of everyone.

The emperor, too, was on the move. He went on eighty-eight royal tours around the country, and was frequently to be seen at military parades, and social functions like balls and wrestling matches. Those of his subjects unable to see him in person could read of his doings in the press, or else buy some of the hundreds of brightly-coloured woodblock prints portraying him. Okubo, noting the public appeal of European royalty, had deliberately taken the emperor out of isolation and given him to the people as their 'father and mother'. It was a wise decision. Admiration for the emperor helped the Japanese to forget their differences, and turn themselves into a nation.

5 The other Japan

While it was a golden age for some Japanese, the Meiji period, like any time of rapid change, was one of much frustration and bewilderment to others. Life in Tokugawa Japan, although far from ideal, had at least been stable and settled. On the whole, people had known their place and were seldom bothered by new and unpredictable situations.

This was no longer so. The people of the Meiji period had to cope with enormous changes. Those who adapted successfully could be satisfied with the new world, but many were left behind. Their dissatisfaction produced an undercurrent of unease in Meiji Japan.

Take the samurai class, for example. The new government had come to power by force. Despite its use of the emperor as a figurehead, it made many enemies, and spent its first twelve months involved in serious fighting in north-eastern Japan. Equally serious revolts were to follow as some of the government's supporters turned against it. Some had expected a tougher line against the foreigners, but instead found them more and more welcomed. Others had hoped that Japan might salvage her dignity by attacking her closest neighbour, Korea, as the first step towards an empire which would include China and Russia. They were disappointed when Okubo and Kido refused. Still more samurai were frightened at the end of the old baronial system, dismayed at the loss of all their old privileges, and appalled when their salaries were stopped.

It was not long before this resentment exploded. In 1873, a leading member of the government resigned in disgust, and went back home to Hizen. There, helped by 5,000 samurai, he launched an armed rebellion against his former colleagues. It was unsuccessful, but other similar incidents, on a smaller scale, followed in 1876, at Kumamoto, Akizuki and Hagi, the latter also led by a former member of the government.

Then came the most menacing of them all. Saigo Takamori, the popular hero of the Restoration, and once one of the four most prominent men in the new government, had stumped back to Satsuma in disgust in 1873. He was an old-fashioned samurai, not a reformer, and he hated what his old friends Okubo and Kido were doing. He had wanted a *coup d'état*, not a revolution.

Back in Satsuma, Saigo proceeded to act as if the reform had never taken place. Samurai still had to wear their swords, and still kept their salaries. Shimazu Tadayoshi, the baron, had gone, but Saigo ruled Satsuma in his place, refusing to pay taxes to the government in Tokyo, and turning a deaf ear to its orders. In 1877, at the head of 42,000 men, he marched north and attacked one of its garrisons.

Okubo, in reply, put 60,000 troops into the field, and it took them seven months, 15,000 casualties, and a mammoth 45

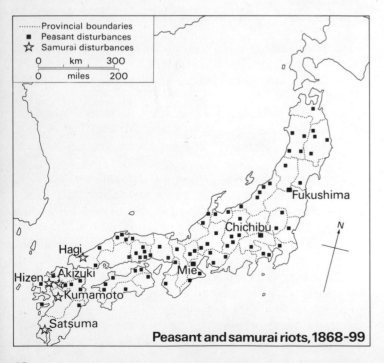

Provincial boundaries
- Peasant disturbances
- ☆ Samurai disturbances

0   km   300
0   miles   200

Fukushima

Chichibu

Hagi

Hizen
Akizuki
Kumamoto

Mie

Satsuma

N

Peasant and samurai riots, 1868-99

million yen (then worth over 20 million dollars) before the rebellion was put down. Saigo himself, at the end, died by the samurai code which had ruled him all his life. He disembowelled himself, and asked a comrade to cut off his head.

Other samurai expressed their unhappiness differently. Some of those excluded from the new government started political movements aimed at winning representation. In the late 1870s a number of small but noisy political parties sprang up, organizing public meetings around the country and drawing up petitions calling for the establishment of a parliament. This was much more effective, in the end, than the rebellions. By 1881 the government had promised them a written constitu-

A speaker at a public meeting, and, below, a voter at the ballot box, casting his vote under the stern eyes of government officials and policemen. The drawings are by the French cartoonist Bigot.

below: Satsuma rebels attacking an imperial garrison, 1877. Saigo Takamori, mounted on a white horse, is directing the attack.

tion, and this constitution, when announced in 1889, allowed for an elected parliament. It was hardly democracy, since only a small number of wealthy men—perhaps 4% of all adult Japanese males—could vote, but at least it was a start.

Samurai were not the only unhappy ones. There were problems in the countryside, too. Peasant rebellions, which had increased in the last years of Tokugawa rule, continued. Between 1869 and 1874 they averaged thirty each year. In one of the largest, in 1876, a riotous army of 10,000 farmers began to burn down government offices and bank buildings in the Mie area east of Osaka. Incidents like this continued well into the 1880s, with as many as 5,000 protesters gathering to burn and plunder at Fukushima in 1882 and Chichibu in 1884.

There were various reasons behind this rural dissatisfaction. After 1873 farmers had to pay their taxes in money, not in goods. This was not popular, nor was the government's plan for a periodical re-assessment of the amount of tax payable on each plot of land. Naturally every farmer thought his particular assessment far too high, and many had little ready cash.

Bad seasons or no, the farmer had to pay his tax, even if it meant going into debt. Many did borrow, and paid dearly for it. In the seven years between 1883 and 1890, over 300,000 farmers, unable to pay their debts, were forced to sell their land, and either move into the cities, or else take work as tenant farmers or as agricultural labourers.

Foreign trade was responsible for much misery in the villages. In many parts of Japan farmers had managed to survive not so much by what they grew as by what they, and their wives and children, produced at home during the long winter evenings. Homespun cotton cloth, rough silk cloth,

left: *Farmers breaking into a storehouse at Mie in 1876.*

right: *Workmen with trays of silk cocoons; a contemporary photograph.*

straw sandals, candles, and many other products of this cottage industry were challenged by goods imported from overseas. Paraffin oil lamps replaced the candles, and the machines of Manchester could produce better cotton goods than any farmer's wife. There were local boycotts of imported goods, but little could be done. The government could not protect its own cottage industries until the treaties were revised.

These tensions provided constant fuel for riots. All that was needed was a spark to set them off. An unpopular local official, for example, or the change from the lunar to the Gregorian calendar (which took place at the beginning of 1873), or a crop failure, or military conscription (since farmers giving up their sons suspected they would never get them back again), or even the appearance of telegraph lines (thought to be products of black magic), was sufficient to bring on a riot.

The countryside was much slower to become Westernized than great cities like Tokyo. But even in Tokyo there were exceptions to the Meiji success story. The capital had its urban poor, living in squalid slums as day-labourers, or rickshaw-men, or rag-pickers. Their lives were short and unhappy, spent in tiny rooms, and sustained by leftovers from army mess halls.

As in the rest of the world, the factory system in Japan meant much misery. Since machines could be worked by women, and

Women labourers at the Ashio copper mine. Environmental pollution from this mine caused violent local opposition, but the government used force to stop demonstrations.

even by children, there was no need to employ men. The majority of factory workers were women, working up to fourteen hours a day in some cases, without regular lunch or rest periods. Child labour was used, discipline was harsh, diseases like tuberculosis and beri-beri were common, and there were some appalling industrial accidents. This was especially so in the coal mines, of course, where 2,000 miners were killed in one explosion in 1878. But it was also true of the factories, for safety precautions were few, and workers were often housed in dormitories above the flimsy wooden sheds in which they worked.

Samurai rebellions, unrest in the countryside, and the misery of the cities all form the other side of Meiji Japan. They were part of the sacrifice Japan had to make when she joined the modern world. Nevertheless, despite individual hardship and confusion, Japan was in many ways a much better place in which to live than it had been before. Some people were still more privileged than others, but a man was no longer limited by what his father had been. There was a legal system and a constitution which gave the Japanese reasonable freedoms and protection. These were considerable achievements.

So was Japan's new confidence with the outside world. By the end of the nineteenth century the unequal treaties were on the way to being altered. The new Japan earned international attention by waging war successfully. Defeating China in 1895 made Japan the strongest nation in East Asia. Defeating Russia ten years later made her one of the strongest nations in the world.

She had come a long way since that day in 1853 when she had been forced – at gunpoint – to join the very risky game of international politics, in which the Western nations held all the cards. Mere survival was an achievement; winning equality was a very great triumph indeed.

Index

Note: All Japanese names appear according to customary Japanese usage, with the family name preceding the personal name.

Acknowledgments

A note on the illustrations in this book.

All the pictures are contemporary; that is, they were drawn or photographed about the time of the events described. Where the pictures are by western artists, the captions make this clear. There are also many pictures by Japanese artists. These are often from coloured prints, a popular form of illustration in Japan until the 1870s, when western methods of illustration took over.

The author and publisher would like to thank the following for permission to reproduce illustrations:
Front cover Gakken Co., Ltd.; back cover, p. 22 Waseda University Library; pp. 5, 6 Nagasaki Prefectural Library; p. 7 Radio Times Hulton Picture Library; pp. 8 (Commodore Perry), 9 (wrestlers), 17, 21, 23, 28, 32 (passenger train), 36 (fashionable ladies), 39 (tabernacle), 46, 47 from S. Konishi *et al.* ed., *Shashinzusetsu Meiji hyakunen no Rekishi*, Vol. II published by Kodansha, Tokyo; pp. 8 (ship), 9 (American sailors) from Oliver Statler *The Black Ship Scroll*, published by Charles E. Tuttle Co., Inc.; pp. 10, 13, 15, 16, 18 (ship at sea), 20, 24 (Saigo Takamori), 25 (Kido Takayoshi), 29, 31, 34 (stamps), 35 (bank and banknote), 36 (reception rooms), 40, 43 (sack of Kumamoto Castle), 44 International Society for Educational Information, Tokyo, Inc.; p. 12 Tokyo National Museum; pp. 14, 32 (steam engine), 41, 45 Mansell Collection; p. 18 (San Francisco harbour), 19 from T. Kimura *Manen Gan'nen Kenbeishisetsu Tobeiki* published by Seicho-sha; pp. 22 (proclamation), 24 (young emperor), 25 (charter oath), 26 (Iwakura Mission), 35 (Iwasaki Yataro), 43 (voting) from K. Kodama *et al.* ed., *Zusetsu Nihonbunkashi*, Vol. II published by Shogakkan, Tokyo; p. 26 (Ito Hirobumi) from K. Nakamura *Itoh Hirobumi* published by Jijitsushinsha, Tokyo; p. 27 Japan Information Centre, London; pp. 30, 37 (London scene) Victoria and Albert Museum; p. 33 Transportation Museum, Tokyo; p. 34 (post boxes) The General Postal Museum of Japan; p. 37 (western style painting) Bijutsu-shippan sha, Tokyo; p. 38 Kokuritsu Shiryo Kan, Tokyo; p. 39 (Ginza) Chuo Koron-sha, Tokyo; p. 48 Illustrated London News, 1912.

The author would also like to thank James Rundle for his advice and criticism.

Maps by Reg Piggott

The Cambridge History Library

The Cambridge Introduction to History
Written by Trevor Cairns

PEOPLE BECOME CIVILIZED   EUROPE AND THE WORLD

THE ROMANS AND THEIR EMPIRE   THE BIRTH OF MODERN EUROPE

BARBARIANS, CHRISTIANS, AND MUSLIMS   THE OLD REGIME AND THE REVOLUTION

THE MIDDLE AGES   POWER FOR THE PEOPLE

The Cambridge Topic Books
General Editor Trevor Cairns

THE AMERICAN WAR OF INDEPENDENCE
by R. E. Evans

LIFE IN THE OLD STONE AGE
by Charles Higham

BENIN: AN AFRICAN KINGDOM AND CULTURE
by Kit Elliott

MARTIN LUTHER
by Judith O'Neill

THE BUDDHA
by F. W. Rawding

MEIJI JAPAN
by Harold Bolitho

BUILDING THE MEDIEVAL CATHEDRALS
by Percy Watson

THE MURDER OF ARCHBISHOP THOMAS
by Tom Corfe

THE EARLIEST FARMERS AND THE FIRST CITIES
by Charles Higham

MUSLIM SPAIN
by Duncan Townson

EARLY CHINA AND THE WALL
by P. H. Nancarrow

POMPEII
by Ian Andrews

THE FIRST SHIPS AROUND THE WORLD
by W. D. Brownlee

THE PYRAMIDS
by John Weeks

HERNAN CORTES: CONQUISTADOR IN MEXICO
by John Wilkes

THE ROMAN ARMY
by John Wilkes

LIFE IN A FIFTEENTH-CENTURY MONASTERY
by Anne Boyd

ST. PATRICK AND IRISH CHRISTIANITY
by Tom Corfe

LIFE IN THE IRON AGE
by Peter J. Reynolds

THE VIKING SHIPS
by Ian Atkinson

The Cambridge History Library will be expanded in the future to include additional volumes. Lerner Publications Company is pleased to participate in making this excellent series of books available to a wide audience of readers.